Table of Contents

Recipe Book
For Feeding
Wild Birds

150 recipes to make your own
suet cakes, seed mixes and other treats
to attract specific birds throughout the seasons

By
Deana Jager

Zosma Publications
Marion, Michigan

Recipe Book
For
Feeding Wild Birds

By
Deana Jager

Published by
Zosma Publications
PO Box 284
Marion, MI 49665
Zosmabooks.com

First Printing May 2007

ISBN 0-9762758-9-9

The information in this book has been carefully researched, and all efforts have been made to ensure accuracy. Zosma Publications and Deana Jager assume no responsibility for any injuries suffered or for damages or losses incurred during the use of or as a result of following this information. It is important to study all directions carefully before taking any action based on the information and advise presented in this book. When using any commercial product, always read and follow label directions. Where trade names are used, no discrimination is intended and no endorsement by Zosma Publications or Deana Jager is implied.
Keep in mind that while it is your intent to feed the birds, putting out feed of any kind can attract other wild animals such as squirrels, raccoon, deer and sometimes even bear.

Feeding Wild Birds

If you feed the birds, it is a good idea to keep your feeders regularly stocked. If you stop feeding the birds, it does not necessarily mean that the birds that visit your feeders will die, however they will have a hard time until they can find new sources of such abundant food. This is significantly true in the winter months and especially during heavy snowfall. The scarcity of food makes it very difficult for little birds and a well-stocked feeder can be what saves their lives at those arduous times. Always be sure to clean away any snow that covers the feed in your feeders so the birds can get to it.

Keeping feeders clean

Because of the high concentration of birds at feeding stations, it is important to keep feeders clean. Feeders need to be kept clean of fungus, mold and droppings. Use a bristle brush and a 10% bleach solution to clean surfaces and disinfect the feeders of any unwanted bacteria. Make sure that you rinse the feeder very well and let it thoroughly dry before refilling with feed. This will help to keep the birds that visit your yard healthy and happy.

Water for the Birds

Offering fresh water for the birds to drink and bath in will actually attract more birds to your yard than a feeding station. Always be sure to keep birdbaths clean by scrubbing them out with a bristle brush and a 10% bleach solution once a week. In the winter months, you can purchase a heater so that little birds will not have the hard time of deriving moisture from the snow and ice. They will also bath in the water in the winter. Many birds enjoy a trickle or spray to clean themselves off with too. Run the sprinkler or put a little fountain in a large pot filled with water on your deck to enjoy the show.

Feeding from your hand

Taming wild birds to eat from your hand is actually easier than you may think. Chickadees and Nuthatches may be some of your first takers. In the winter, when food is scarce, is the best time to entice them. Empty out all feeders except one. In the early morning, when birds are hungriest, sit very still in a chair about 3-feet away from the feeder. When you first sit down the birds will probably fly away but remain seated until they return, usually within a half an hour, to feed again. Stay sitting still while they feed for another half an hour.

The next day, position your chair right next to the feeder and repeat the same method, waiting for them to return to feed at the feeder tray.

On the third day, empty your feeder tray and fill with a less desirable seed mix. Fill your hand with temping sunflower seeds, rest your open hand on the feeder, and stay still. They may not eat from your hand just yet, but be patient.

The fourth day, empty your feeder and offer only from your hand resting on the feeder; you should get a taker this time. Continue this procedure for a few more days, and then try standing if you wish.

Once you have regular visitors, move away from the feeder a few feet at a time. Carry some favorite seeds and nuts in your pocket when you are in the yard in case a friendly bird comes to you for food.

BLACKBIRDS
Redwing Blackbird, Crow, Raven

Ravens and crows are omnivorous and can easily find food. Serve food directly on the ground or in a low feeder tray at the far end of your yard. Gradually move the food closer to where you would like to view them.

Pink & Black Pancakes

1c. Strawberries   1 c. black oil sunflower seeds
Pancake mix to make 10-12 pancakes.

Use fresh, frozen or dried strawberries. If using fresh or frozen berries, reduce water content in recipe by 1/3. Prepare pancakes according to directions on box, including strawberries and sunflower seeds. To serve, crumble on the ground.

Blackbird's Favorite Foods
Baked Goods
Bones, marrow & meat
Berries
Carrion
Corn
Dog Food
Eggs, raw or cooked
w/shell
Fish
Fruit
Insects
Leftovers
Meat, raw or cooked
Pasta, cooked
Suet
Table scraps

Blackbird Bonanza

2 lb. chunk raw suet
2 c. high fat hamburger, cooked or raw
3 c. cooked pasta
6 egg shells
2 c. hulled sunflower seeds
2 c. unsalted peanuts, chopped
2 c. raisins or other dried fruit

Grind suet in a meat grinder. Grind eggshells into small pieces. Mix all ingredients together and combine well. Serve only what will be consumed in one day on the ground or low table feeder. Store the remainder in freezer.

8

BLUEBIRDS

These beautiful songbirds are a prize in anyone's yard. They are easily tamed and if you are patient, you can train them to eat from your hand.

Berry Bluebird Salad

Bluebirds will love the variety of berries in this offering.

1 lb. raw suet	*½ c. raisins or currants*
1 c. blueberries	*½ c. figs*
1 c. raspberries	*½ c. cherries*
½ c. wild sumac berries	*¾ c. bayberry, juniper,*
1 c. chopped nuts	*or holly berries*

Grind suet in a meat grinder. Use fresh, frozen or dried berries. Chop up figs, cherries and raisins. If you are using frozen berries, thaw them first and drain excess juices if the outside temperature is above freezing. Combine all ingredients. Serve on open tray feeder or scattered on the ground

Bluebird's Favorite Foods

Baked Goods
Bayberries
Blackberries
Blueberries
Dogwood Berries
Juniper Berries
Mealworms
Peanuts & Peanut Butter
Pine Nuts
Raisins
Raspberries
Suet

Go Nuts for Berries

Kids will love to get there hands into making this fun, Bluebird tempting treat!

½ lbs. raw suet	*½ c. cranberries*
1 c. natural, chunky peanut butter	*½ c. strawberries*
½ c. peanuts	*½ c. raspberries*
½ c. pine nuts	*½ c. cornmeal*

Grind or cut up suet into small pieces and combine with peanut butter. Chop up berries and nuts, and then add cornmeal. Use your hands to mix all ingredients together. Crumble daily portions into a feeding tray. Store the remainder in the freezer.

Blueberry Bird Betty

2 c. whole-wheat flour
1 c. brown sugar
1 c. blueberries
½ c. rendered suet

½ c. chopped peanuts
½ c. water
½ tsp. baking powder
1 tsp. baking soda

Mix flour, baking powder, soda and nutmeats. Set aside. Boil sugar, raisins, shortening and water for 5 minutes. Add liquid to dry ingredients. Spoon mixture into well-greased 8"x8" cake pan. Bake at 350° for 20-25 minutes. Cut into pieces, place on feeder tray or ground feeder.

Peanut Butter Bluebird Meal

1 lb. raw suet
1 c. natural, chunky peanut butter
1 c. whole-wheat flour
1 c. peanuts

1 c. applesauce
½ c. raisins
3 c. cornmeal

Chop suet into large pieces and put into food processor, add raisins, 1 cup of cornmeal and peanuts then chop all into small pieces. Transfer to a large bowl and add applesauce, peanut butter and flour. Mix, adding more flour if need, to achieve a crumbly consistency. Serve daily portions in tray feeders. Freeze the rest in plastic bags.

Bluebird Grub

2 lb. chunk raw suet
2 c. hulled sunflower seeds

2 c. raisins
2 c. unsalted peanuts

Grind suet in a meat grinder. It will come out looking like grubs that bluebirds love. Mix all ingredients together combine well. Serve only what will be consumed in one day on a table feeder. Store the remainder in freezer.

Bluebird Breakfast

Bluebirds will enjoy this homemade cereal.

½ lb. raw suet
1 c. blueberries ,fresh, frozen or dried
½ c. chopped peanuts

1 c. oatmeal
½ c. cornmeal
½ c. cooking oil

Cut or grind suet into small pieces. Mix all the ingredients in a large bowl and serve on an open tray feeder.

Blueberry Cornmeal Crumble

1 pkg. jiffy corn bread mix
¼ c. fresh blueberries

¼ c. cornmeal
¼ c. chopped raisins.

Prepare corm bread according to package directions, adding the berries, cornmeal and raisins. Crumble onto a table feeder.

Pink Bluebird Suet

1 c. rendered suet
1 c. natural, chunky peanut butter
2 c. cornmeal
1 c. wild sumac berries

1 c. hull sunflower seed
1 c. pine nuts
½ c. raspberries
1 c. whole-wheat flour

Melt suet in a saucepan over low heat. Add peanut butter, stirring until melted and well blended. Mix the rest of the ingredients together in a large bowl. Allow the suet-peanut butter blend to cool until slightly thickened, and then stir it into the mixture in the bowl. If necessary, add more flour to reach a firm consistency. Fill chosen container, then freeze. Remove from container; serve and keep remainder in a bag in the freezer.

BLUE JAY

Jamin' Jay Suet

1 c. rendered suet
1 c. natural, chunky peanut butter
½ c. grape jam
2 hardboiled eggs, with shells

2 slices whole wheat bread
1 c. peanuts, chopped
½ c. meat scraps
1 c. corn meal

Melt suet in a saucepan over low heat. Add peanut butter, stirring until melted and well blended. In a food processor, chop up meat scraps, hard-boiled eggs (leave the shells on), bread and peanuts then transfer to a large bowl. Mix in corn meal and sand. Allow the suet-peanut butter blend to cool until slightly thickened, and then stir it into the mixture in the bowl. If necessary, add more cornmeal to reach a firm consistency. Fill chosen container, then freeze. Remove from container; serve and keep remainder in a bag in the freezer.

> **Blue Jay's Favorite Foods**
> Acorns
> Baked Goods
> Corn
> Crackers
> Eggs, cooked
> Fruit, fresh or dried
> Grapes
> Mealworms
> Meat Scraps
> Nuts
> Peanuts & Peanut Butter
> Pine Nuts
> Suet

Jay's Favorite Mix

2 c. crushed, corn flakes
½ lb. chunk raw suet
½ c. chopped peanuts
½ c. cracked or cooked corn

1 c. grapes
1 c. meat scraps
¼ c. cooking oil
½ c. pine nuts

Put the chunk of suet through a meat grinder then transfer to a large bowl. Crush up the corn flakes (use stale ones if you like). Chop up grapes and peanuts. Cut meat scrapes (cooked or raw) into small pieces. Add all ingredients to large bowl and mix well. Serve only what will be consumed in one day on a table feeder. Store the rest in a marked bag in the freezer.

BUNTING

Berry Bunting Treat

½ c. granola cereal
½ c. blue or black berries
½ c. elderberries
½ c. raspberries

½ c. chopped nuts
1 c. wild bird seed
¼ c. millet

Mix all the ingredients together and serve on a table feeder.

Bunting's Favorite

½ c. chopped peanuts
½ c. fruit & nut cereal
1 c. thistle (niger) seed
1 c. sunflower seeds

½ c. corn flakes
1 c. rapeseed
½ c. millet
1 c. canary seed

Mix all ingredients together and serve on a table feeder.

Bunting's
Favorite Foods
Canary Seed
Corn Flakes
Blackberries
Elder berries
Fruit & nut cereals
Millet
Mixed Seeds
Nuts, chopped
Peanuts, chopped
Rapeseed
Raspberries
Thimbleberries
Weed seeds

CARDINALS

Cardinal Apple Suet

1 c. rendered suet
1 c. natural peanut butter
2 medium apples

1 c. black-oil sunflower seeds
1 c. chopped peanuts
1 c. oatmeal (uncooked)

Melt suet in a saucepan over low heat. Add peanut butter, stirring until melted and well blended. Dice up apples (including core & seeds) into small pieces and transfer to a large bowl. Add sunflower seeds, peanuts and oats. Mix well. Allow the suet-peanut-butter blend to cool until slightly thickened, and then stir it into the mixture in the bowl. If necessary, add more oatmeal to reach a firm consistency. Fill a 8"x8" pan and freeze until firm. Cut into four 4"x4" pieces and serve in suet cages. Keep remainder in a bag in the freezer.

Cardinal's Favorite Foods
Apples
Baked Goods
Blackberries
Corn
Grapes
Mellon and squash seeds
Millet
Mulberries
Oats
Peanuts & Peanut Butter
Raisins
Safflower seeds
Suet

Cardinal Seed Mix

10 lb. black-oil sunflower seeds
10 lb. hulled sunflower seeds
10 lb. safflower seeds
5 lb. unsalted pumpkin seeds

5 lb. raisins
5 lb. peanuts
5 lb. cracked corn

Mix all ingredients together and serve on a low table feeder or on the ground. Store seed mix in a cool place in a container with a secure lid.

Cardinal Super Treat

1 lb. chunk raw suet
2 c. grapes
2 c. bread or other baked goods
1 apple

1 c. wild sumac berries
1 c. black-oil sunflower seeds
1 c. safflower seeds
½ c. raisins

Put suet through a meat grinder then crumble into a large bowl. Chop grapes and apple in to small pieces and add to bowl. Tear bread into small pieces, add with the rest of the ingredients to the bowl, and mix well. Serve on a table feeder or on the ground. Store the rest in a marked plastic bag in the freezer.

Berry Nutty Salad for Cardinals

1 c. black-oil sunflower seeds
½ c. chopped peanuts
½ c. oatmeal (uncooked)
½ c. unsalted pumpkin or squash seeds

1 c. black berries
1 c. wild sumac berries
1 c. red grapes
1 medium red apple

Dice apple (include core and seeds) and grapes into small pieces. A food processor works well for this. Transfer to a large bowl and add the remaining ingredients. Serve on a low table feeder or on the ground.

Day Old Treat for Cardinals

4 c. of any day old baked good (bread, bagels, doughnuts ect.)
1 c. sunflower seeds, any kind
1 c. raisins

Break baked goods into small beak-size pieces and mix with other ingredients. Serve on a low table feeder or on the ground.

CEDAR WAXWING

Cedar's Suet Cake

2 c. rendered suet   1 c. raisins
1 large apple

Melt suet in a saucepan over low heat. Cut whole apple (core and seeds) into small cubes. Steam the raisins in small amount of water to plump them up. Put apple pieces, seeds and raisins into 8"x8" foil pan. Allow the suet to cool until slightly thickened, and then pour over apples and raisins then mix. Put in the freezer until firm. Cut into four 4"x4" pieces and serve in suet cages. Store what remains in a marked plastic bag in the freezer.

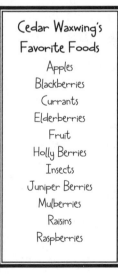

Cedar Waxwing's Favorite Foods

Apples
Blackberries
Currants
Elderberries
Fruit
Holly Berries
Insects
Juniper Berries
Mulberries
Raisins
Raspberries

Waxwing Fruit Salad

1 med apple   1 c. raspberries
1 c. blackberries   1 c. elderberries
1 c. raisins   1 c. strawberries

Use fresh, frozen & thawed or dried berries. Dice whole apple (core & seeds) and strawberries into small pieces. Mix and serve on a table feeder.

CHICKADEES

Nutty Doughnut Cakes

1 c. rendered suet
1 c. peanut butter
½ c. brown sugar

6 c. stale cake doughnuts
1 c. chopped peanuts
½ c. whole-wheat flour

Melt suet in a saucepan over low heat. Add peanut butter, stirring until melted and well blended. Break doughnuts up into pieces and mix together with peanuts. Allow the suet-peanut butter blend to cool until slightly thickened, and then stir it into the mixture in the bowl. If necessary, add more flour to reach a firm consistency. Fill a 8"x8" pan and freeze until firm. Cut into four 4"x4" pieces and serve in suet cages. Keep remainder in a bag in the freezer.

Chickadee Chow

1 c. rendered suet
1 c. natural peanut butter
1 c. hulled sunflower seed
1 c. pecans or walnuts.

1 c. pine nuts
1 c. peanuts
½ c. coconut flakes
½ c. raisins

Chickadees
Favorite Foods
Acorns
Baked Goods
Coconut
Cornmeal
Hamburger, raw
Mealworms
Nuts
Peanuts & Peanut
Butter
Pine Nuts
Suet
Sunflower Seeds

Melt suet in a saucepan over low heat. Add peanut butter, stirring until melted and well blended. Mix the remaining ingredients together in a large bowl. Allow the suet-peanut butter blend to cool until slightly thickened, and then stir it into the mixture in the bowl. Fill chosen container, then freeze. Remove from container; serve and keep remainder in a plastic bag in the freezer.

COWBIRD

Cowbird's Favorite Suet

1 c. rendered suet
1 c. natural peanut butter
2 slices whole wheat bread
1 c. cracked corn

½ c. meat scraps
1 c. corn meal
1 c. peanuts
½ c. pine nuts

Cowbird's Favorite
Foods

Acorns
Baked Goods, breads &
pasties
Cornmeal
Cracked corn
Hamburger, raw
Mealworms
Nuts
Peanuts & Peanut Butter
Pine Nuts
Suet

Melt suet in a saucepan over low heat. Add peanut butter, stirring until melted and well blended. In a food processor, chop up meat scraps, bread and peanuts then transfer to a large bowl. Mix in corn meal, cracked corn and pine nuts. Allow the suet-peanut butter blend to cool until slightly thickened, and then stir it into the mixture in the bowl. If necessary, add more cornmeal to reach a firm consistency. Fill a 8"x8" pan and freeze until firm. Cut into four 4"x4" pieces and serve in suet cages. Keep remainder in a bag in the freezer.

Cowbird Seed Mix

10 lb. cracked corn
10 lb. hulled sunflower seeds

5 lb. peanuts
1 lb. pine nuts

Mix all ingredients together and serve on a low table feeder or on the ground. Store seed mix in a cool place in a container with a secure lid or in a brown paper bag.

GOLDFINCH

Finch Seed Mix

1 lb. canary seed	½ lb. white millet
1 lb. hemp seed	½ lb. red millet
2 lb. thistle (niger) seed	½ lb. flaxseed
1 lb. black-oil sunflower seeds	½ lb. chopped peanuts

Mix all ingredients together and store in a cool place in a container with a secure lid or in a brown paper bag.

Finch's Favorite Suet

2 c. rendered suet	1 cup millet
2 c. thistle (niger) seed	½ c. bread crumbs
1 c. hulled sunflower seeds	1 c. flaxseed

Melt suet in a saucepan over low heat. In a large bowl mix remaining ingredients. Allow the suet to cool until slightly thickened, and then stir it into the mixture in the bowl. If necessary, add more breadcrumbs to reach a firm consistency. Pour into four empty tuna or cat food cans. Sprinkle with a pinch of sand. Refrigerate to harden. Attach to post or tree.

> **Goldfinch's Favorite Foods**
> Aster
> Bachelor's-Button seed
> Canary Seed
> Coneflower Seed
> Coreopsis Seed
> Cosmos Seed
> Flaxseed
> Goldenrod Seed
> Grass Seed
> Lettuce Seed
> Millet
> Niger, (Thistle seed)
> Peanut hearts
> Rapeseed
> Suet
> Sunflower seed, Esp. Black oil
> Zinnia seed

GRACKLE

Grackle Goodie Crumble

2 c. yellow cornmeal

2 c. whole wheat flour

1 c. dried milk

4 tsp. baking powder

4 eggs including shells

1 c. canned mixed fruit

1 c. cracked corn

1 c. hulled millet

4 c. warm water

2 c. frozen corn (thawed)

Mix all dry ingredients together. Add wet ingredients. Grease two 9"x12" pans and bake at 425° for 25 minutes. Cool completely on a wire rack then crumble into medium size pieces. Serve on a table feeder or hang in a mesh bag. Store the remainder in a marked plastic bag in the refrigerator.

Grackle's
Favorite Foods

Acorns

Apples

Bayberries

Beechnuts

Baked Goods

Canary seeds

Corn

Fruit

Peanuts

Seeds

Sunflower seeds

Grackle Seed Mix

1 lb. dried apples

5 lb. canary seeds

5 lb. cracked corn

5 lb. peanuts

5 lb. sunflower seeds

5 lb. safflower seeds

Chop the dried apples in a food processor into small pieces. Combine all ingredients and store in a cool place in a container with a secure lid.
Serve on a table feeder or on the ground.

GROSBEAKS

Grosbeak Goodie Mix

5 lb. cracked corn   *5 lb. white millet*
5 lb. sunflower seeds   *3 c. dried cherries*
5 lb. unsalted peanuts   *2 lb. raisins*
4 c. dried figs, chopped up *2 lb. wheat berries*

Chop the dried figs in a food processor into small pieces. Combine all ingredients and store in a cool place in a container with a secure lid.
Serve on a table feeder or on the ground.

Grosbeak Grub

2 lb. chunk raw suet   *2 c. cracked corn*
2 c. sunflower seeds   *2 c. unsalted peanuts*
1 c. wild sumac berries   *1 c. figs, chopped up*

Grind suet in a meat grinder. Crumble the ground suet into a large bowl then. Add remaining ingredients and mix well. Serve only what will be consumed in one day on a table feeder. Store the remainder in freezer.

Grosbeak's Favorite Foods

Acorns
Blackberries
Cherries, fresh or dried
Common ragweed
Corn
Crackers
Dogwood Berries
Elderberries
Figs
Fruit
Millet
Peanuts
Safflower seeds
Seeds
Sumac
Sunflower Seeds
Virginia creeper berries
Wheat
Wild Grapes

HOUSE (PURPLE) FINCH

Finch's Favorite Suet

2 c. rendered suet
2 c. thistle (niger) seed
1 c. hulled sunflower seeds

1 cup millet
½ c. bread crumbs
1 c. hulled pumpkin seeds

Melt suet in a saucepan over low heat. In a large bowl mix remaining ingredients. Allow the suet to cool until slightly thickened, and then stir it into the mixture in the bowl. If necessary, add more breadcrumbs to reach a firm consistency. Pour into four empty tuna or cat food cans. Sprinkle with a pinch of sand. Refrigerate to harden. Attach to post or tree with a large nail.

> **House Finch's Favorite Foods**
> Bread Crumbs
> Canary seed
> Crushed eggshells
> Fruit
> Melon seeds
> Millet
> Nectar
> Niger (Thistle Seed)
> Oranges
> Peanut hearts
> Safflower seeds
> Salt
> Sunflower seeds, any kind
> Suet

Finch Seed Salad Mix

1 can mixed fruit, drained
2 c. hulled sunflower seeds
6 egg shells, crushed
1 c. thistle (niger) seed
1 c. pumpkin seeds

1 medium orange
2 c. canary seeds
2 c. safflower seeds
2 stale bagels
2 c. peanuts

Put peanuts, pumpkin seeds and bagel into a food processor and chop into small pieces. Transfer to a large bowl. Peel and dice the orange. Drain canned fruit and add, along with the diced orange, to bowl. Add the remaining ingredients and mix well. Serve on a table feeder. Store the remainder in a container in the refrigerator and use within a few days.

HUMMINGBIRDS

Hummingbird Nectar

A ratio of 1:4 is used to make this hummingbird nectar. You can make multiples of this recipe in accordance with the number of feeders you put out or store extra servings in the refrigerator. This recipe contains about 21% sucrose, favored by North American hummingbirds.

4 c. well or spring water   *1 c. white cane sugar.*
7 ice cubes, ½ tray equaling approx. 1 cup of water

Bring water to a boil. Add sugar. Stir and remove from heat. Stir in ice cubes and let "nectar" cool completely before serving in feeders. Store in refrigerator for up to 2 weeks or freeze for several months.

JUNCOS

Junco Seed Mix Meal

2 slices whole-wheat bread
2 c. hulled sunflower seeds
2 c. safflower seeds
1 c. thistle (niger) seed
1 c. mixed wild flower seeds

1 c. cracker crumbs
2 c. canary seeds
1 c. corn meal
2 c. white millet
2 c. peanuts

Put peanuts, bread and crackers into a food processor and chop into small pieces. Transfer to a large bowl. Add the remaining ingredients and mix well. Serve on a table feeder. Store the remainder in a container in the refrigerator and use within a few days.

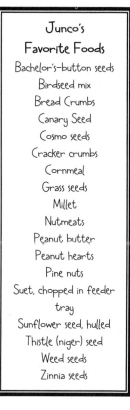

Junco's
Favorite Foods

Bachelor's-button seeds
Birdseed mix
Bread Crumbs
Canary Seed
Cosmo seeds
Cracker crumbs
Cornmeal
Grass seeds
Millet
Nutmeats
Peanut butter
Peanut hearts
Pine nuts
Suet, chopped in feeder tray
Sunflower seed, hulled
Thistle (niger) seed
Weed seeds
Zinnia seeds

Junco Jelly Delight

2 lb. chunk raw suet
2 c. hulled sunflower seeds
¼ c. grape jelly
1 c. cracked corn

2 c. raisins
2 c. unsalted peanuts
1 c. cornmeal
¾ c. millet

Grind suet in a meat grinder then crumble into a large bowl. Mix in the remaining ingredients until well combined. Serve only what will be consumed in one day on a table feeder. Store the remainder in freezer.

MOCKINGBIRDS

Mockingbird Munch

1 can mixed fruit, drained
4 slice whole-wheat bread
½ c. peanut butter
½ c. corn flakes or other cereal

½ c. meat scraps
½ c. cornmeal
¼ c. cooking oil

Combine all ingredients until mixed. Break up clumps and chill. Serve on a table feeder. Store the remainder in a container in the refrigerator and use within a few days.

Mockingbird Meaty Muffins

1 c. cornmeal
¾ c. raisins
1 c. whole-wheat flour
1 tsp. baking soda

1 c. breadcrumbs
½ c. meat scraps
½ c. cooking oil
¾ c. water

Combine cornmeal, flour, breadcrumbs and soda in a medium bowl. Add raisins and meat scraps. Pour in oil and water. Mix well and spoon into muffin tins. Bake at 350° for 15 minutes. Serve on feeder or hang in mesh bags.

Mockingbird's
Favorite Foods
Baked goods
Cereal
Chopped Suet
Corn
Crackers
Dogwood berries
Fruit, fresh or dried
Grapes
Hamburger, raw
Hawthorn berries
Holly berries
Leftovers
Mealworms
Meat scraps
Millet
Oranges

NUTHATCH

Nuthatch Nibbles

1 c. rendered suet
1 c. natural, chunky peanut butter
½ c. pine nuts
2 c. popped popcorn

2 slices whole-wheat bread
1 c. peanuts, chopped
1 c. sunflower seeds
1 c. corn meal

Melt suet in a saucepan over low heat. Add peanut butter, stirring until melted and well blended. In a food processor, chop up bread and peanuts then transfer to a large bowl. Mix in remaining ingredients. Allow the suet-peanut butter blend to cool until slightly thickened, and then stir it into the mixture in the bowl. If necessary, add more cornmeal to reach a firm consistency. Fill a 8"x8" pan and freeze until firm. Cut into four 4"x4" pieces and serve in suet cages. Keep remainder in a bag in the freezer.

Nuthatch's
Favorite Foods
Baked goods
Corn
Elderberries
Melon seeds
Milo
Nuts
Peanuts & Peanut Butter
Pine Nuts
Rapeseed
Suet
Sunflower seeds
Virginia creeper berries
Wheat

Nuthatch Seed Mix

5 lb. cracked corn
5 lb. sunflower seeds
5 lb. unsalted peanuts
4 c. raw pumpkin seeds

5 lb. white millet
3 c. currents
2 lb. pine nuts
2 lb. wheat berries

Combine all ingredients and store in a cool place in a container with a secure lid. Serve on a table feeder or on the ground.

ORIOLES

Oriole Fabulous Fruit Salad

1 c. cherries	2 c. diced pears
2 oranges	1 c. blackberries
1 c. raspberries	2 c. diced peaches
1 c. grape jelly	½ c. cornmeal

Use fresh, frozen & thawed, or canned fruit. Cut oranges, cherries, peaches and pears into small beak-size pieces. Toss all the fruit together in a large bowl. Heat the jelly in the microwave for 30 sec. to 1 min. until thin. Stir the jelly then pour over fruit. Mix until the fruit is well coated. Sprinkle cornmeal over mixture and stir again. Serve in a shallow dish on a separate table feeder. Refrigerate the remainder in a container and use within a few days.

PB&J for Orioles

4 slices whole wheat bread	grape Jelly
natural peanut butter	½ c. cornmeal

Pour the cornmeal onto a plate. Spread a thick coating of peanut butter onto one slice of bread and press, peanut butter side down, into the cornmeal. Coat a second slice of bread with grape jelly and press, jelly side down, into cornmeal. Put the slices together to make a sandwich. Repeat with other two slices of bread. Use a knife to cut into ½ in. chunks. Serve on a feeder tray.

Oriole's Favorite Foods

Apples
Baked goods
Beechnuts
Berries, esp. mulberries
Blackberries, blueberries
And huckleberries
Cornmeal
Elderberries
Figs
Fruit
Jelly
Millet
Nectar
Oranges
Peaches
Peanut butter
Pears
Peas, fresh, dried or frozen
Suet, chopped

REDPOLL

Rolling Redpoll Balls

2 c. rendered suet
1 c. thistle (niger) seeds
½ c. black-oil sunflower seeds
½ c. hulled sunflower seeds

½ c. millet
½ c. canary seeds
½ c. grass seed
½ c. whole-wheat flour

When you purchase the grass seed, make sure that it is all natural and not chemically treated in any way. Melt suet in a saucepan over low heat. Mix remaining ingredients together in a large bowl. Allow the suet to cool until slightly thickened, and then stir it into the mixture in the bowl. If necessary, add more flour to reach a firm consistency. Form in to balls freeze until hard. Serve on a table feeder or hang in a mesh bag. Store the rest in a plastic bag in the freezer.

Redpoll's
Favorite Foods
Bread
Birdseed mix
Canary seed
Grass seed
Millet
Sunflower seed, black oil or
hulled
Weed seeds, such as
Ragweed, pigweeds
Smartweed and
Suet
Sunflower seeds, hulled
Thistle (niger) seed
Lamb's-quarter

Redpoll Feeder Mix

1 lb. Wild birdseed
2 lb. canary seed
5 lb. hulled sunflower seeds

5 lb. white millet
5 b. thistle (niger) seed

Combine all ingredients and store in a cool place in a container with a secure lid. Serve on a table feeder or on the ground.

ROBINS

Fruit Pasta for Robins

1 lb. chunk raw suet
1 medium apple

½ c. raisins
1 c. cooked pasta

Grind suet in a meat grinder. It will come out looking like grubs that robins love. Mix all ingredients together combine well. Scatter on the ground. Serve only as much as will be consumed in one day. Store the remainder in freezer.

Robin Cherry Bread

2 c. whole wheat flour
½ c. sugar
shells)
2 tsp. baking powder
¼ c. cornmeal
chopped

¼ c. melted butter
2 eggs (include

1 c. milk
1 c. cherries,

Robin's
Favorite Foods
Apples
Bayberries
Berries
Baked goods
Breadcrumbs
Cherries, fresh or dried
Corn, cracked
Crackers, crumbled
Grapes
Hawthorn berries
Holly berries
Mealworms
Raisins

Stir together flour, cornmeal, sugar, and baking powder; add cherries. Whisk eggs with milk and add melted butter. Add egg mixture to fruit and flour mixture, stirring with fork until well combined. Crush eggshells into small pieces and stir into mixture. Pour into greased 9x5x3 inch loaf pan and bake at 350° for about 55 minutes. Cool on a wire rack, then slice off a piece and crumble onto a table feeder. Store the remainder in the refrigerator.

SPARROW

Sparrow's Favorite Foods
Baked goods
Birdseed
Blackberries
Blueberries
Breadcrumbs
Canary seeds
Cereal
Cherries, fresh or dried
Chick scratch
Corn, cracked
Crackers, crumbled
Elderberries
Evening primrose seeds
Foxtail grass seeds
Grapes
Grass seeds
Millet
Milo
Nuts
Oats
Peanuts
Rapeseed
Safflower seeds
Seeds of garden flower
Suet, chopped
Thistle (niger) seeds
Weed seeds

Splendid Sparrow Cakes

4 halves of stale bagel	1 c. rendered suet
½ c. chopped peanuts	1 c. peanut butter
½ c. safflower seeds	½ c. raisins

Melt suet in a saucepan over low heat. Add peanut butter, stirring until melted and well blended. Break bagels up into pieces and mix together with nuts and raisins. Allow the suet-peanut butter blend to cool until slightly thickened, and then stir it into the mixture in the bowl. Mix well to achieve a firm consistency that will hold together. Trim the top off a ½-gallon cardboard milk or orange juice carton and pack all the mixture in. Refrigerate until firm, and then with a serrated knife, slice a piece off the size to fit in suet cage, remove cardboard and serve. Keep remainder in a bag in the freezer and thaw slightly to cut another serving as needed.

Sparrow Seed Mix

5 lb. safflower seeds	5 lb. canary seed
5 lb. peanuts	5 lb. thistle seed
5 lb. white millet	5 lb. cracked corn
5 lb. mixed bird seed	2 lb. raisins

Combine all ingredients and store in a cool place in a container with a secure lid. Serve on a table feeder or on the ground.

STARLINGS

Starling Stampede

6 egg shells, washed & dried
2 c. cracked corn
2 c. dry dog food
4 slices whole-wheat bread

½ lb. raw suet
1 c. raisins
1 c. meat scraps
1 c. cooked pasta

In a food processor chop up bread, pasta, eggshells and meat scraps. Transfer to a large bowl and add remaining ingredients. Serve on a table feeder and store the remainder in a marked plastic bag in the freezer.

Starling Jiffy Pleaser

2 pkg. jiffy corn bread mix
½ c. chopped apples

½ c. meat scraps
½ c. wild birdseed

Prepare cornbread according to package directions, adding meat craps and fruit. Bake as directed. Cool on a wire rack then crumble on the ground away from songbirds.

Starling's
Favorite Foods
Apple Peelings
Baked goods
Birdseed
Bones, w/meat & marrow
Breadcrumbs
Cereal
Corn, cracked
Crackers, crumbled
Dog food
Fruit
Holly berries
Leftovers
Meat scraps
Millet
Milo
Pasta, cooked
Oats
Raisins
Suet, chopped
Wheat

TANAGERS

Tasty Tanager Suet

1 c. rendered suet
1 c. natural peanut butter
1 c. white millet
1 c. raisins

½ c. whole-wheat flour
1 c. cornmeal
1 c. hulled sunflower seeds
2 c. whole-wheat bread pieces

Melt suet in a saucepan over low heat. Add peanut butter, stirring until melted and well blended. Mix the rest of the ingredients together in a large bowl. Allow the suet-peanut butter blend to cool until slightly thickened, and then stir it into the mixture in the bowl. If necessary, add more flour to reach a firm consistency. Fill a 8"x8" pan and freeze until firm. Cut into four 4"x4" pieces and serve in suet cages. Keep remainder in a bag in the freezer.

Tanager's
Favorite Foods
Baked goods
Blackberries
Breadcrumbs
Elderberries
Fruit
Fruit & nut cereals
Mealworms
Millet
Mulberries
Nuts
Raspberries
Salmonberries
Suet
Sumac
Sunflower seeds, hulled
Thimbleberries
Wine berries

Tanager Feeder Treat

1 can mixed fruit
1 c. white millet
1 c. hulled sunflower seeds
2 c. granola cereal

1 c. blackberries
1 c. chopped nuts
1 c. raisins
1 c. raspberries

Combine all ingredients and serve on a separate table feeder. Store the remainder in a marked container in the refrigerator and use within a few days.

THRUSHES

Thrush's Favorite Foods

Bayberries
Birdseed
Blackberries
Blueberries
California Peppertree berries
Cherries, fresh or dried
Dogwood Berries
Elderberries
Evening primrose seeds
Figs
Grapes
Greenbrier berries
Mealworms
Millet
Milo
Mulberries
Peanuts
Peanut butter
Raisins
Rosehips
Spicebush berries
Strawberries
Suet, chopped
Virginia creeper berries

Blackberry Bread for Thrushes

1 ½ c. apple juice
¾ c. rolled oats
¼ molasses
4 c. whole-wheat flour
¾ c. blackberries
1 pkg. yeast
¼ c. warm water
3 tbs. butter

Bring apple juice to a boil. Add oatmeal, blackberries and molasses. Set aside to cool. Sprinkle yeast over warm water in a large bowl, and stir until dissolved. Stir oatmeal mixture into yeast. Stir in 2 cups flour. Add remaining flour, and blend with a mixer or with hands. Cover and let rise for 30 minutes in a warm place. Grease a 9"x5"x3" loaf pan. Beat dough 25 strokes with a sturdy spoon, and then spread in the pan. Smooth the top with a greased spatula. Cover and let rise until about 1 inch from top of the pan. Bake at 425° for 45 minutes. Cool on a wire rack. Tear into small pieces to serve on a feeder tray.

Seed Mix for Thrushes

1 c. wild birdseed
1 c. peanuts
½ c. dried figs
¾ c. blackberries
1 c. raisins
1 c. blueberries

Mix all the ingredients together and serve on a table feeder. Store the remainder in a marked container in the refrigerator. Use within a few days.

TUFTED TITMOUSE

Tufted Titmouse Feeder Mix

1 c. leftover cereal
½ c. shredded coconut
1 c. safflower seeds
1 c. peanuts

1 c. meat scraps
1 c. dried apples
½ c. raisins
½ c. dried cherries

Chop dried apples, pecans, peanuts and meat scraps into small pieces. Transfer to a large bowl and add remaining ingredients. Mix all the ingredients together well and serve on a table feeder. Store the remainder in a marked plastic bag in the refrigerator and use within a few days.

Titmouse Suet Treat

1 c. rendered suet
1 c. natural peanut butter
4 stale doughnuts
½ c. whole-wheat flour
½ c. chopped pecans

1 c. sugar
1 finely diced apple
½ c. raisins
½ c. cornmeal
½ c. dried cherries

Tufted Titmouse's Favorite Foods

Acorns
Apples
Baked goods & pastries
Bayberries
Beechnuts
Cereal
Cherries, fresh or dried
Coconut
Corn, cracked
Crackers, crumbled
Meat scraps
Nuts
Peanuts
Peanut butter
Pine nuts
Safflower seeds
Suet
Sunflower Seeds

Melt suet in a saucepan over low heat. Add peanut butter, stirring until melted and well blended. Break doughnuts up into pieces and mix together with remaining ingredients. Allow the suet-peanut butter blend to cool until slightly thickened, and then stir it into the mixture in the bowl. Mix well to achieve a firm consistency that will hold together. Pour into a greased 9"x5" bread pan and refrigerate until firm, then with a serrated knife, slice a piece off the size to fit in suet cage. Keep remainder in a bag in the freezer.

TOWHEE

Wowhee Towhee Treat

2 lb. chunk raw suet
1 c. hulled sunflower seeds
1 c. blueberries
1 c. oatmeal, uncooked

1 c. blackberries
1 c. peanuts
1 c. cracked corn

Grind suet in a meat grinder. It will come out looking like grubs that birds love. Mix all ingredients together. Serve only what will be consumed in one day on a table feeder. Store the remainder in freezer.

Towhee's
Favorite Foods
Acorns
Barleys
Baked goods
Bayberries
Birdseed
Blackberries
Blueberries
Corn, cracked
Flaxseed
Fruit
Grass seeds
Millet
Oats
Peanuts
Suet, chopped
Sunflower seed
Thistle (niger) seed

Tufted Titmouse Feeder Mix

5 lb. wild birdseed
5 lb. white millet
5 lb. sunflower seeds
5 lb. thistle seeds
1 lb. oatmeal, uncooked

5 lb. peanuts
5 lb. cracked corn
2 lb. raisins
2 lb. barley
2 lb. flaxseed

Mix all ingredients together and serve on the ground or a low table feeder. Store the remainder in a cool place in a container with a secure lid.

WOODPECKERS

Wooing Woodpecker Suet

1 c. rendered suet
1 c. natural peanut butter
1 c. dried figs, chopped
½ c. whole-wheat flour
1 c. shredded coconut

½ c. chopped pecans
1 c. cracked corn
1 c. peanuts
1 c. pine nuts
½ c. dried cherries

Melt suet in a saucepan over low heat. Add peanut butter, stirring until melted and well blended. Mix together with remaining ingredients in a large bowl. Allow the suet-peanut butter blend to cool until slightly thickened, and then stir it into the mixture in the bowl. Mix well to achieve a firm consistency that will hold together. Pour into a greased 9"x5" bread pan and refrigerate until firm, then with a serrated knife, slice a piece off the size to fit in suet cage. Keep remainder in a bag in the freezer.

Woody Woodpecker Treat

½ c. rendered suet
½ c. natural peanut butter

1 c. wild bird seed
½ c. meat scraps

Use a 1'x3" diameter log or piece of untreated wood. Drill several 1" holes in it. Screw an "eye" into the top to hang with a piece of twine. Melt suet and peanut butter in a pan. Let cool slightly then add birdseed and meat scraps and mix well. Push the soft suet in the holes and hang on a feeder pole or from a tree branch.

Woodpecker's Favorite Foods

Acorns
Almonds
Berries
Cherries, fresh or dried
Coconut
Corn
Dogwood berries
Elderberries
Figs
Grapes
Hazelnuts
Hickory nuts
Holly berries
Mealworms
Meat scraps
Mulberries
Nectar
Peanuts
Peanut butter
Pecans
Pine nuts
Suet
Sumac berries
Sunflower seeds
Walnuts

42

WREN

Cheeseburger Bread for the Birds

2 c. whole-wheat flour
3 tsp. baking powder
¾ c. meat scraps, cooked
¾ c. American cheese, grated

1 c. milk
¼ c. cooking oil
1 c. chopped nuts, any kind
1 egg (reserve shells)

Stir together flour and baking powder. Chop meat scraps into small pieces and grate cheese, mix and add to flour mixture. Mix milk, oil and eggs to combine. Pour into dry ingredients, and stir until moist. Crush eggshells into small pieces and add to mixture. Pour into a greased bread pan and bake at 400° for 20 min. To serve, crumble small portions onto a table feeder. Store the remainder in the refrigerator.

Rolling Wren Suet

4 slices whole wheat bread
1 ½ c. rendered suet
½ c. chopped peanuts

½ c. dried apples
1 c raisins
½ c. sunflower seeds

Melt suet in a saucepan over low heat. Mix together with remaining ingredients in a large bowl. Allow the suet to cool until slightly thickened, and then stir it into the mixture in the bowl. Mix well to achieve a firm consistency that will hold together. Pour into a large piece of waxed paper. Bring up the sides and press into a ball. Refrigerate until firm then serve on a feeder tray.

Wren's
Favorite Foods
Apples, halved or chopped
Baked goods
American cheese
Elderberries
Fruit
Leftovers
Mealworms
Meat scraps
Nuts
Peanuts
Peanut butter
Suet
Sunflower seeds

Suet

Suet is raw beef fat that comes in large chunks and is available at your local supermarket. You may want ask the meat department for beef trimmings and if they will grind it for you. You can also grind it at home with a hank-crank or electric meat grinder. It comes out looking like the grubs that birds love. You can keep suet feeders up all year round; however, it is an ideal food to serve birds in the winter. Not only will it not spoil, but it also provides the extra calories that birds need to sustain warmth and health in the cold winter months. Your consideration will be well rewarded with a wide array of grateful visitors. Bluebirds, cardinals, chickadees, kinglets, juncos, mockingbirds, nuthatches, thrashers, titmice, woodpeckers and wrens are just some of the eager dinner guest that will arrive when suet is served. In the migratory months, you may attract an even broader array of birds, including the yellow-bellied sapsucker and flickers. In the summer months, suet will melt and turn rancid in the hot sun, so serve it in the shade and put out only what will be consumed within a few days.

Other Fats

Use an empty coffee can to collect excess fats from beef, bacon grease, chicken fat and other meat drippings and fat. Store the container in the freezer and use to make some of the recipes in this book.

Rendering Suet

Rendering suet gets the meat particles out of the fat. Repeating the rendering process makes it harder and it will not melt as easily, once formed into a mold. Process fat in a meat grinder or food processor or you can chop it up with a knife. Heat fat over a medium-low heat until it turns to liquid. Pour liquefied fat through a fine sieve to strain out particles. Let cool, then reheat, and strain again. When the suet is still liquid, use it to make the recipes in this book, then pour into chosen mold or form in to various shapes. Cool and store in a plastic bag in the freezer.

Suggested ways to mold and serve rendered suet

- Disposable aluminum baking tins or cups
- Reuse the containers from store-bought suet cakes
- ½ gallon, cardboard milk cartons, cut the lid off and fill. Slice into servings to fit suet cages.
- From a mold with heavy-duty aluminum foil or cardboard.
- Yogurt containers
- Cake pan, lined with plastic wrap, then cut into squares for suet cages.
- Bread loaf pan, lined with plastic wrap, slice to fit into suet cages.
- Pie tins, cut into pie slices and serve.
- Form a log over skewer
- Hang in a mesh onion bag.
- Smear onto the bark of trees.
- Fill a pinecone with suet
- Make a log feeder and fill it.

Suet Cakes & Meals

Summer Suet

This recipe does not melt as quickly in warmer weather.

2 c. suet
2 c. quick oats

2 c. cornmeal
1 ½ c. white flour

Melt suet in a saucepan over low heat. Add peanut butter, stirring until melted and well blended. Mix the rest of the ingredients together in a large bowl. Allow the suet-peanut butter blend to cool until slightly thickened, and then stir it into the mixture in the bowl. Mix thoroughly. If necessary, add more flour to reach a firm consistency. Fill chosen container, then freeze. Remove from container; serve and keep remainder in a bag in the freezer.

Birdie Breakfast

2 c. rendered suet
2 c. natural, chunky peanut butter
3 c. quick oats
4 c. water
½ c. chopped nuts

3 c. cream of wheat
3 c. cornmeal
½ c. raisins
1 c. whole-wheat flour

Melt suet in a saucepan over low heat. Add peanut butter, stirring until melted and well blended. In another pan, cook oatmeal in water for 2 minutes. Remove from heat and add in suet-peanut butter blend, mix well. Add cornmeal, cream of wheat and flour. Cool until you can handle it. Shape into cakes that will fit in your feeder or press into chosen molds and refrigerate until firm. Serve and keep remainder in a marked bag in the freezer.

Sweet Peanut Butter Treat

A high protein, high energy treat

1 c. suet
1 c. natural, crunchy peanut butter
2 c. corn meal
½ c. chopped peanuts

2 c. quick oats
1 c. whole-wheat flour
¼ c. brown sugar

Melt suet in a saucepan over low heat. Add peanut butter, stirring until melted and well blended. Mix the rest of the ingredients together in a large bowl. Allow the suet-peanut-butter blend to cool until slightly thickened, and then stir it into the mixture in the bowl. If necessary, add more flour to reach a firm consistency. Fill a 8"x8" pan and freeze until firm. Cut into four 4"x4" pieces and serve in suet cages. Keep remainder in a bag in the freezer.

Fruit n' Bread Bars

1 lb suet
1 c. natural peanut butter
½ loaf of whole wheat bread
½ c. whole-wheat flour
½ c. cornmeal

1 c. sugar
1 finely diced apple
½ c. raisins or dried blueberries
½ c. canned cherries
½ c. chopped pecans

Melt suet in a saucepan over low heat. Add peanut butter, stirring until melted and well blended. Drain cherries very well. Tear bread in to small pieces. In a large bowl, mix cherries, flour and bread together until all liquid is absorbed, and then add the rest of the ingredients. Allow the suet-peanut butter blend to cool until slightly thickened, and then stir it into the mixture in the bowl. If necessary, add more flour to reach a firm consistency. Cover a 9"x5" bread pan with plastic wrap and press mixture in. Refrigerate until firm but not too hard. Slice into "bars" and return to refrigerator until hard. Serve in suet cage. Store remainder in a bag in the freezer

Seed Pizza with Fruit Toppings

This is a fun one! Kids will love to create this "Pizza" for the birds.

2 lb. suet

2 c. natural peanut butter

4 eggshells (washed)

½ c. figs, dates, or raisins

½ c. dried Turkish apricots

½ c. dried pineapple chunks

1 apple

1 c. wild birdseed

1 c. rolled oats

½ c. whole-wheat flour

¾ c. peanuts

¾ c. slivered almonds

Melt suet in a saucepan over low heat. Add peanut butter, stirring until melted and well blended. Allow the suet-peanut butter blend to cool until slightly thickened. Reserve 1/3 of dried fruit and nuts and chop up the rest into small beak-size pieces. Be sure to use the Turkish apricots because they contain no sulfur. Grind the eggshells up fine. Combine eggshells, fruit, nuts, flour in a large bowl, and mix well. Work all into suet-peanut butter blend and mix thoroughly, until thick. Press onto a greased cookie sheet. While it is still warm, press the reserved dried fruit and nuts into pizza for the "Toppings". Refrigerate until hard, then cut with a pizza cutter and serve. Keep remainder in a marked bag in the freezer.

Berry Tasty!

1 c. rendered suet

1 c. peanut butter

½ c. dried cranberries

½ c. dried blueberries

½ c. raisins

½ c. cornmeal

½ c. almonds, chopped

½ c. whole-wheat flour

Melt suet in a saucepan over low heat. Add peanut butter, stirring until melted and well blended. Mix the rest of the ingredients together in a large bowl. Allow the suet-peanut butter blend to cool until slightly thickened, and then stir it into the mixture in the bowl. If necessary, add more flour to reach a firm consistency. Fill chosen container, then freeze. Remove from container; serve and keep remainder in a bag in the freezer.

Berry, Berry Tasty!

4 c. rendered suet
½ c. raspberries
½ c. strawberries
½ c. blueberries
½ c. cranberries
½ c. holly, juniper berries or other bush berry

½ c. wild sumac berries
½ c. elderberries
1 c. unsalted nuts, any kind
1 c. quick oats
½ c. corn meal
1 c. whole-wheat flour

You can use fresh, frozen, canned, dried and/or wild berries for this recipe. Be sure to thaw and thoroughly drain all frozen berries. Fresh berries should be wild or organic, otherwise wash in mild soapy water, then rinse very well and drain and let dry. Melt suet in a saucepan over medium-low heat. Chop nuts into small pieces and toss with berries, quick oats, corn meal and flour in a large bowl. Allow the suet to cool until slightly thickened, and then stir it into the mixture in the bowl. If necessary, add more flour to soak up any juices and mixture reaches a firm consistency. Fill a 8"x8" pan and freeze until firm. Cut into four 4"x4" pieces and serve in suet cages. Keep remainder in a bag in the freezer.

Super Seedy Suet Cakes

2 c. rendered suet
½ c. hulled sunflower seed
½ c. flax seed
½ c. cantaloupe or watermelon seeds

½ c. safflower seeds
½ c. thistle seeds
½ c. pumpkin or squash seeds

Melt suet in a saucepan over low heat. Allow it to cool thoroughly, and then reheat it. Mix the seeds together in a large bowl. Allow the suet to cool until slightly thickened, and then stir it into the mixture in the bowl. Mix thoroughly. Cool until you can handle it. Shape into cakes that will fit in your feeder or press into chosen molds. Refrigerate until hard. Serve and keep remainder in a marked bag in the freezer.

Fat-Belly Bird Cakes

1 c. rendered suet
1 c. peanut butter
½ c. dried fruit (raisins, apples, ect.)

6-8 stale cake doughnuts
½ c. chopped peanuts
½ c. hulled sunflower seeds

Melt suet in a saucepan over low heat. Add peanut butter, stirring until melted and well blended. Break doughnuts up into pieces and mix together with nuts and fruit. Allow the suet-peanut butter blend to cool until slightly thickened, and then stir it into the mixture in the bowl. Mix well to achieve a firm consistency that will hold together. Trim the top off a ½-gallon cardboard milk or orange juice carton and pack all the mixture in. Refrigerate until firm, then with a serrated knife, slice a piece off the size to fit in suet cage, remove cardboard and serve. Keep remainder in a bag in the freezer and thaw slightly to cut another serving as needed.

Matt's Meaty-Bird Pie

Best served only in the winter, because of the meat.
You can put this out in warmer weather but cook the meat and
only serve small portions at a time so that it won't get rancid.

2 c. rendered suet
½ c. unseasoned bread crumbs
½ c. whole-wheat flour

1 c. meat trimmings, scraps or fat
1 c. ground beef, cooked to raw
½ c. real bacon bits

Melt suet in a saucepan over low heat. Mix the rest of the ingredients together in a large bowl. Allow the suet to cool until slightly thickened, and then stir it into the mixture in the bowl. If necessary, add more flour to reach a firm consistency. Line a pie plate with plastic wrap and fill with mixture, then freeze. Remove and slice like a pie. Serve one slice at a time on a table feeder or hang in a mesh bag. Keep remainder in a bag in the freezer.

Rosie-Berry Bird Cake

2 c. rendered suet
1 c. natural, chunky peanut butter
1 c. wild rose hips
1 c. raspberries
1 c. blueberries

1 c. raisins
1 c. quick oats
1 c. cornmeal
½ c. whole-wheat flour
1 c. wild birdseed

Mix ingredients and add enough bacon drippings to hold it all together. Shape into balls or press into pinecones. Freeze leftovers.

"Suet-Cream" Cone

2 c. rendered suet
2 c. peanut butter
¼ c. molasses
½ c. unsalted nuts, any kind
1 c. raisins
12 ice cream cake cones

1 lb. oatmeal
1 c. cornmeal
½ c. hulled sunflower seeds
½ c. whole-wheat flour
5 c. wild bird seed
½ c. powdered milk

18 feet twine & several small sticks cut into 2-inch sections.

Set aside wild birdseed. Melt suet in a saucepan over low heat. Add peanut butter, stirring until melted and well blended. Coarsely chop nuts and mix together with the rest of the ingredients in a large bowl. Allow the suet-peanut butter blend to cool until slightly thickened, and then stir it into the mixture in the bowl. If necessary, add more flour to reach a firm consistency. Cut twine into 12, 18-inch lengths and tie a small twig to the end to prevent cone from sliding off. Poke a hole in the bottom of each cone. Thread the twine through the hole, so that the stick lays flat against the bottom of the cone. Gently pull twine taunt and fill the cone ¾ of the way full with birdseed. Then, with your hands, form a 3-inch ball of suet mixture around the twine, and gently press into cone, like an ice cream cone. Then coat each one with wild birdseed. Chill then hang outside.
Yields 12-3inch cones.

Birdie Bread Pudding

2 c. rendered suet
½ c. brown sugar

4-6 stale large bagels
1 c. raisins

Melt suet in a saucepan over low heat. Break bagels up into pieces and mix together with raisins and brown sugar in a large bowl. Allow the suet to cool until slightly thickened, and then stir it into the mixture in the bowl. Fill chosen container, or press into shapes or modes. You could also line pudding cups with plastic wrap and fill with "bread pudding". Freeze until firm then serve only what will be consumed within a few days. Keep remainder in a bag in the freezer.

Gone Nutty Cakes

Chickadees, jays, nuthatches, titmice and woodpeckers

2 c. rendered suet
2 c. natural, nutty peanut butter
1 c. peanuts
½ c. almonds
½ c. chestnuts
½ c. pine nuts

1 c. acorn hearts
½ c. walnuts
½ c. pecans
¾ c. quick oats
½ c. whole-wheat flour
¾ c. sugar

Choose plain, unsalted nuts. Use stale leftovers from the holidays or your cooking cupboard. Combine all nuts and chop coarsely in food processor or blender. Melt suet in a saucepan over low heat. Add peanut butter, stirring until melted and well blended. Mix the rest of the ingredients together in a large bowl. Allow the suet-peanut butter blend to cool until slightly thickened, and then stir it into the mixture in the bowl. If necessary, add more flour to reach a firm consistency. You can spread it onto tree trunks or tree limbs for easy feeding or spread it in a 1-inch deep baking pan and refrigerate until hardened. Cut into squares to fit your feeder. Keep remainder in a bag in the freezer.

Apple Suet Muffins

2 c. rendered suet

2 c. chopped apples, include core & seeds

½ c. brown sugar

1 c. stale doughnut, broken-up

2 ½ c. rolled oats

1 c. hulled sunflower seeds

Melt suet in a saucepan over low heat. In a large bowl, break up the stale doughnuts then mix together with the rest of the ingredients in a large bowl. Allow the suet to cool until slightly thickened, and then stir it into the mixture in the bowl. Press into greased muffin tins and freeze until firm. Serve on a table feeder or hang in mesh bag. Store the remainder in a marked plastic bag in the freezer.

Peanut butter & Jelly Sandwich

3 c. rendered suet

1 c. natural, chunky peanut butter

1 c. peanuts

4 slices bread

1 c. wild birdseed mix

½ c. grape jelly

1 c. raisins

1 c. corn meal

½ c. whole-wheat flour

You will need to use two saucepans for this recipe. In one saucepan, melt 1 cup suet over low heat. Add peanut butter and peanuts, stirring until melted and well blended. In the other saucepan, melt 2 cups of suet over low heat, then add jelly, raisins, cornmeal and flour. Toast the bread. Mix the rest of the ingredients together in a large bowl. Allow the suet blends to cool until slightly thickened. Cover one side of two slices of toast with a thick coating of the suet-jelly blend. Sandwich the coated sides together. Cover the whole outside (front & back) of the sandwich with suet-peanut butter blend. Press both sides of the sandwich into wild birdseed to cover, repeat for a second sandwich. Place sandwiches on a wax paper lined cookie sheet and freeze until hard. Serve on feeder tray or in mesh bag. Keep one sandwich in the freezer until ready to use.

Bird Gone Dog Cakes

Blackbirds, jays, mockingbirds, robins, thrashers, thrushes, starlings, wrens

3 c. rendered suet
1 c. peanut butter
1 can dog food
1 c. dry dog food or biscuits, chopped up
½ c. quick oats

½ c. crushed peanuts
½ c. cracked corn
½ c. cornmeal
½ c. sunflower seeds
½ c. whole-wheat flour

Melt suet in a saucepan over low heat. Add peanut butter, stirring until melted and well blended. Chop up dry dog food and peanuts and mix together with the rest of the ingredients in a large bowl. Allow the suet-peanut butter blend to cool until slightly thickened, and then stir it into the mixture in the bowl. If necessary, add more flour to reach a firm consistency. Fill chosen container, then freeze. Remove from container; serve and keep remainder in a bag in the freezer.

Popcorn Peanut Butter Balls

Blackbirds, jays, mockingbirds, robins, thrashers, thrushes, starlings, wrens

2 c. rendered suet
2 c. natural, chunky peanut butter
7 c. popped popcorn, unsalted
½ c. cracked corn

½ c. cornmeal
½ c. crushed peanuts
½ c. brown sugar
½ c. whole-wheat flour

Melt suet in a saucepan over low heat. Add peanut butter, stirring until melted and well blended. Mix remaining ingredients together in a large bowl. Allow the suet-peanut butter blend to cool until slightly thickened, and then stir it into the mixture in the bowl. If necessary, add more flour to reach a firm consistency. Form in to balls freeze until hard. Serve on a table feeder or hang in a mesh bag. Store the rest in a plastic bag in the freezer.

Sweet Cherry Suet

2 c. rendered suet

1 c. chunky peanut butter

1 c. canned or dried cherries

1 c. rolled oats

½ c. sugar

1 c. hulled sunflower seed

1 c. crushed graham crackers

½ c. whole-wheat flour

1 tbs. fine sand

Melt suet in a saucepan over low heat. Add peanut butter, stirring until melted and well blended and reserve. If using canned cherries drain well and mix with the rest of the ingredients in a large bowl. Allow the suet-peanut butter blend to cool until slightly thickened, and then stir it into the mixture in the bowl. If necessary, add more flour to reach a firm consistency. Fill chosen container or press into a plastic lined cookie sheet and freeze until hardened. Cut into squares to fit suet cages. Keep remainder in a bag in the freezer.

A Hearty Helping

Chickadees, crows, jays, magpies,
starlings, titmice, woodpeckers & wrens

¼ lb. cooked hamburger

1 c. cornmeal

2 c. cooked beans

¾ c. brown sugar

¾ c. peanut butter

¼ c. powdered milk

3 eggshells, washed

¾ c. chopped fresh or dried fruit

2 c. oatmeal or wheat flakes

½ c. oat or wheat bran

2 tbs. wheat germ oil

Cook the hamburger. Grind up the eggshells and mix all ingredients together. Serve on a separate table feeder.

Coconut Boats

1 whole coconut	½ c. raisins
2 c. rendered suet	½ c. crushed gram crackers
1 c. natural, chunky peanut butter	½ c. flaxseed
1 c. cornmeal	1 part brown sugar
½ c. hazelnuts	1 tbs. fine sand

Split coconuts in half. Drill a hole on each side of both halves to thread a wire or twin through for hanging. Melt suet in a saucepan over low heat. Add peanut butter, stirring until melted and well blended and reserve. Mix with the rest of the ingredients in a large bowl. Allow the suet-peanut butter blend to cool until it starts to thickened, and then stir it into the mixture in the bowl. Fill coconut halves with mixture and hang from trees.

Super Cereal Suet

2 c. rendered suet	4 c. leftover or stale cereal
2 c. natural, chunky peanut butter	1 c. raisins or other dried fruit
½ c. unsalted, chopped peanuts	½ c. jiffy corn meal mix
½ c. hulled Sunflower.	

Melt suet in a saucepan over low heat. Add peanut butter, stirring until melted and well blended. Mix the rest of the ingredients together in a large bowl. Allow the suet-peanut butter blend to cool until slightly thickened, and then stir it into the mixture in the bowl. If necessary, add more cornmeal mix to reach a firm consistency. Fill chosen container, then freeze. Remove from container; serve and keep remainder in a bag in the freezer.

No Suet Cakes

4 c. natural chunky peanut butter

2 c. water

1 tbs. butter

½ c. hulled sunflower seeds

2 c. rolled oats

½ c. cornmeal

½ c. raisins

1 tbs. sugar

½ c. whole-wheat flour

1 tbs. sand

Boil water. Add butter, sugar, oatmeal and raisins. Cook one minute and stir in remaining ingredients. Press into molds and serve on feeder tray.

Popcorn Pleaser

½ c. rendered suet or lard

½ c. natural, peanut butter

7 c. popped popcorn

½ c. peanuts, chopped or whole

½ c. raisins or currants

½ c. cornmeal

½ c. black-oil sunflower seed

Pop popcorn and pour into a large metal bowl. Melt suet or lard and peanut butter in a pan over medium heat and drizzle over popcorn. Add the rest of the ingredients and mix well until the popcorn is thoroughly covered. Serve on a table feeder or in a large mesh bag (like an orange bag).

Grub-ish Grub

2 lb. chunk raw suet

2 c. high fat hamburger, cooked or raw

6 stale bagels or other bread

2 c. hulled sunflower seeds

2 c. unsalted peanuts

2 c. raisins or other dried fruit

Grind suet in a meat grinder. It will come out looking like grubs that birds love. Run bagels through a food processor or blender to chop into small pieces. Mix all ingredients together combine well. Serve only what will be consumed within a day and store the remainder in the freezer.

Fruit & Veggies

Very Berry Bonanza

½ c. blueberries
½ c. raspberries
½ c. cherries
1 c. rolled oats

½ c. sumac berries
½ c. cranberries
½ c. strawberries

Use fresh, frozen or dried berries. Fresh berries should be organic or wild, otherwise wash in a mild soapy water and rinse twice, *very* well. If you are using frozen berries, thaw them first and drain excess juices if the outside temperature is above freezing. The oatmeal will absorb excess juices as well. Combine all ingredients. Serve on open tray feeder or scattered on the ground. In the winter, just toss frozen berries together and serve. This is a nice way to provide extra vitamins in the leaner months.

Birdie Fruit Kabob

1 apple
1 orange
1 nectarine
½ c. large grapes

¼ cantaloupe
8 whole, dried figs
1 c. pineapple rings
1 c. fresh strawberries

You'll need a "kabob skewer" that can be purchased at a bird feed supply store. You can make your own by screwing a 1-foot piece of ¼-inch dowel onto a 10" x 10" square of ¾-inch plywood. Wash all the fruit well and cut large pieces. Thread onto the skewer and securely screw the rod into the holder and hang it on a feeder pole

Feathered Friends Fruit Salad

1 apple	1 orange
1 mango	1 plum
¼ cantaloupe	1 peach
1 nectarine	1 c. grapes

Cut fruit into small pieces. Serve only what will be consumed in a few hours to prevent spoiling or mold. Put out on table feeders or hang in a mesh bag. Refrigerate any extra and use all with a few days.

Apple Delight

4 apples, core & seeds	¼ c. walnuts
1 c. raisins	½ c. unsalted peanuts
2 tbs. sugar	2 tbl. wheat germ

Wash apples with soapy water and rinse very well. Put whole apples and the rest of the ingredients into food processor and pulse to chop into small pieces. Be careful not to over process. Serve on a table feeder.

Bird Beans

Blackbirds, cardinals, crows, doves, grackles, grosbeaks, grouse, jays, quail, pheasants, sparrows.

1 c. dried peas	2 c. cracked corn
1 c. red lentils	1 c. split peas
1 c. black oil sunflower seeds	

Combine all and serve on table feeders or scattered on the ground.

Mashed Potato Patties

1 c. rendered suet
1 c. mashed potatoes
½ c. raisins

½ c. cornmeal
½ c. mixed bird seed
½ c. whole-wheat flour

Melt suet in a saucepan over low heat. Mix the rest of the ingredients together in a large bowl. Allow the suet-peanut butter blend to cool until slightly thickened, and then stir it into the mixture in the bowl. If necessary, add more flour to reach a firm consistency. Form into patties with your hands or cut the top off a ½ gallon, cardboard milk container and fill. Freeze until firm. If you use the cardboard container, just slice off a piece big enough to fit in a suet cage and remove the cardboard before serving. You can put the patties in a suet cage too. Keep remainder in a bag in the freezer.

Nutty Fruit Salad

1 lb. raw suet
½ c. natural, chunky peanut butter
½ c. almonds
½ c. walnuts
½ c. pecans
½ c. peanuts
1 c. cracked corn
½ c. figs
*Use all unsalted nuts.

½ c. cranberries
1 apple, quartered
1 c. strawberries
½ c. dried figs
1 c. papaya
½ c. mixed birdseed
½ c. black oil sunflower seed.
½ c. cooking oil

Cut suet into large chunks and put in a food processor. Pulse 1to 2 times to chop into smaller pieces. Add all the nuts, apple, figs and raisins. Chop it all up into small pieces. Transfer to a large bowl. Chop up the papaya and add remaining ingredients. Chill for ½ hour, then crumble into a table feeder or hang in a fine mesh bag. Serve only what will be consumed in a short period and store the rest in a marked plastic bag in the refrigerator. Use all within a few days.

Dried Apples

This recipe is just as good for people too! Make several batches at once.
This saves energy and there will be enough apples for birds & people to share.

5 small apples   *2 c. water*
3 tbs. lemon juice

Core but do not peel the apples. Cut apples into 1/8" thick pieces. Combine lemon juice and water. Pour over mixture over the apples. Toss to coat the apples well. Place apple slices on a wire rack, on cookie sheet and bake at 200° for 3 ½ - 4 hours. They should be leathery, not crispy. Turn off the oven and leave the apples in the oven overnight or for about 8 hrs. Chop into small pieces and use in recipes throughout this book. Note: Instead of throwing away bruised or old apples, save them to dry.

Dried Fruit n' Nut Mix

Bluebirds, catbirds, purple finches, black-headed and rose-breasted grosbeaks, mockingbirds, robins, thrashers and wrens.

3 c. raisins or currants   *1 c. prunes or figs*
1 c. dried cherries   *2 c. peanuts*
2 c. chopped dried apples   *1 c. pumpkin, squash or melon seeds*
1 c. dried cranberries   *1 c. pine nuts*
½ c. cornmeal

Choose unsalted nuts and seeds. Combine peanuts and pumpkin or melon seeds in a food processor and chop into beak-size bites. Do the same with dried apples and prunes, adding cornmeal to prevent sticking. Combine all ingredients, serve and store in a paper sack in cool, dry place.

For Fledglings

Berry Cheesy Blend (for fledglings)

1 c. small curd cottage cheese

¼ c. raspberry jelly

¾ c. blueberries

¾ c. strawberries

Stir jelly into cottage cheese. Dice up the strawberries into small pieces. Mix berries together with cottage cheese mixture and set out in shallow containers. Serve only what will be consumed within a day and store the rest in a marked container in the refrigerator.

Peanut Butter & Jelly for Fledglings

1 c. organic quick oats

½ c. natural, creamy peanut butter

2 c. water

¼ c. grape jelly

½ c. grapes

Bring water to a boil then add oats. Remove from heat and stir in peanut butter. Dice the grapes into small pieces. Add grapes and jelly to oatmeal mixture then stir until well combined. Put in the refrigerator until completely cooled. Serve small portions in low containers. Store the remainder in a marked container in the refrigerator.

Fledgling Suet

The softer and smooth texture easier for young birds to swallow.

2 c. rendered suet   ½ c. grape jelly
1 c. natural, creamy peanut butter   ½ c. sugar

Melt suet over low heat and allow to cool until it begins to thicken. Stir in peanut butter, jelly and sugar. Pour into containers and set out on feeder tray.

Baby Bread

4 slices of whole wheat bread   2 tbs. sugar
½ c. milk

Stir sugar and milk until dissolved. Cut bread into small pieces and soak in the sweetened milk until it is absorbed. Serve in a small, shallow container on feeding tray.

Nectars

Hummingbirds benefit the minerals contained in well or spring water, which is preferred over distilled or chlorinated water. If you have to use chlorinated water, fill a pitcher with water and leave it uncovered on the counter or in the refrigerator over night. Chlorine is a gas and will evaporate out of the water.

Do not use brown sugar, raw (turbinado) sugar, honey, Jell-O, or fruit in hummingbird feeders or nectar. Raw sugar (turbinado) contains about five times as much iron as white sugar. Hummingbird's small bodies hoard iron and even a slight excess of iron can poison them. Honey ferments rapidly when diluted with water and can kill hummingbirds. There is also no need to add red food coloring to the nectar. Syrup solutions can spoil quickly in warm weather, especially in direct sunlight, so hang feeders from the branch of a shade tree or in any shaded area.

Hummingbird Nectar

The ratio for making hummingbird nectar is 1:4. You can make multiples of this recipe in accordance with the number of feeders you put out. This recipe contains about 21% sucrose, favored by North American hummingbirds.

4 c. well or spring water   *1 c. white cane sugar.*
7 ice cubes (½ tray equaling approx. 1 cup of water)

Bring water to a boil. Add sugar. Stir and remove from heat. Stir in ice cubes and let "nectar" cool completely before serving in feeders. Store in refrigerator for up to 2 weeks or frozen for several months.

Oriole Nectar

A ratio of 1:6 is used to make oriole nectar. You can make multiples of this recipe in accordance with the number of feeders you put out.

5 c. well or spring water   *1 c. white cane sugar*
7 ice cubes (½ tray equaling approx. 1 cup of water)

Bring water to a boil. Add sugar. Stir and remove from heat. Stir in ice cubes and let "nectar" cool completely before serving in feeders. Store in refrigerator for up to 2 weeks or frozen for several months.

Seed, Cereal & Nut Mixes

Feeding wild birds is fun and easy. Seed mixes can be stored in a large, clean garbage cans or galvanized

Top 10 favorite foods of wild birds:

Based on a study published by the National Wildlife Federation

1. Black-oil sunflower seeds
2. Black-striped sunflower seeds
3. Hulled sunflower seeds
4. White millet
5. Peanuts and peanut hearts
6. Red millet
7. Golden Millet
8. Canary Seed
9. Corn, whole, cracked & milled
10. Thistle (Niger) seed

Various Foods
Wild Birds Like to Eat:

Acorns	Melon seeds
Almonds	Millet
Apples, dried	Oats, oatmeal
Baked goods, bread, doughnuts, cake	Potatoes, cooked
Beechnuts	Pasta, cooked
Berries, dried	Peanuts, whole, chipped
Bones	Peas, dried
Cereal	Pecans
Cheese	Pine nuts
Coconut	Pumpkin Seeds
Corn, whole, cracked, meal, popped	Raisins
Currants	Rice, cooked
Egg shells	Safflower seeds, hulled, whole
Flax seed	Squash seeds
Hazelnuts	Sunflower seeds, any kind
Hickory nuts	Thistle
Insects	Walnuts
Legumes	Wheat

Ultimate Birdie Bonanza

This is for the ultimate bird connoisseur.

5 lbs. black-oil sunflower seeds

5 lbs. sunflower seeds, hulled

5 lbs. safflower seeds, hulled

5 lbs. thistle(niger) seed

5 lbs. whole peanuts

5 lbs. cracked corn

2 lbs. pumpkin (or melon) seeds

2 dz. egg shells, coarsely ground

3 lbs. peanuts, chopped

2 lbs. hazelnuts, chopped

2 lbs. pine nuts

2 lbs. canary seed

3 lbs. raisins

2 lbs. dried cranberries

2 lbs. figs, chopped

2 lbs. dried apples, chopped

Choose unsalted, raw seeds and nuts. Chop up the figs and dried apples ½ lb. at a time in a food processor. Do the same with the hazelnuts, peanuts, and 1 lb of pumpkin seeds. Eggshells should be rinsed and dry, and can be ground all at once. Mix all ingredients together and store in a large container with a secure lid. Yields: 50 pounds of bird feed.

Birdseed Goodies

2 c. whole wheat bread crumbs

¼ c. cornmeal

½ c. whole wheat flour

½ c. sugar

½ c. shredded cheese

2 c. natural peanut butter

1 c. unsalted nuts, chopped

4 apples

1 c. raisins

1 c. wild bird seed

1 lb. raw suet

1 can mixed fruit, drained

Grind suet in a meat grinder and crumble into a large bowl. Chop the apples into small pieces, include seeds and core, and add to bowl. Add remaining ingredients and mix well. If necessary add bacon drippings if it is too crumbly. Refrigerate until firm them crumble onto a table feeder or hang in a mesh bag.

Cardinal Seed Mix

10 lbs. black-oil sunflower seeds
10 lbs. hulled sunflower seeds
10 lbs. safflower seeds
10 lbs. unsalted peanuts, chopped or whole

5   lbs. cracked corn
2 ½ lbs. dried apples, chopped
2 ½ lbs. raisins

Mix all ingredients well. Store in a cool place, in a container with a secure lid. Yield: 50 lb. birdseed

Bacon, Eggs & Toast for the birds

Blackbirds, chickadees, jays

4 slices stale bread
Bacon, crumbled or other meat scraps

2 eggs, hardboiled
2 c. wild birdseed

In a food processor, chop up the whole egg (with shells) and bacon into small pieces. Tear bead into small pieces and put in a large bowl. Add the chopped eggs, bacon and birdseed. Mix well. Serve on a low table feeder or on the ground.

Gourmet Seed Mix

10 lbs. black-oil sunflower seeds
5 lbs. black-striped sunflower seeds
5 lbs. hulled sunflower seeds
5 lbs. peanut hearts or peanuts

5 lbs. thistle (niger) seed
5 lbs. white millet
5 lbs. cracked corn
5 lbs. chicken layer mesh

Mix all ingredients and store in a cool place in a container with a secure lid. Yield: 45 lbs.

Wild Game Bird Seed Mix

3 lbs. lentils
1 lb. dried white peas
1 lb. dried green peas
1 lb. oat groats
1 dz. egg shells

2 lbs. chicken layer mesh
2 lbs. cracked corn
1 lb. buckwheat
1 lb. soybean seeds

Grind eggshells into small pieces. Combine all ingredients and offer on the ground. Make sure there is near by cover so that birds can retreat if threatened.

Hanging Bird Treat

Mockingbirds, cedar waxwings and wrens.
These hold together better in cooler weather.

2 packets of unflavored gelatin
¼ c. hot water
1 c. black-oil sunflower seeds
1 c. cracked corn
1 c. safflower seeds
twine

1 c. chopped peanuts
1 c. chopped walnuts
1 c. raisins
1 c. dried apples, chopped
1 c. dried figs, chopped

Mix the packets of gelatin with water and stir until dissolved. Chop dried apples and figs into small pieces in a food processor. Combine all nuts and dried fruit in a large bowl and add the dissolved gelatin. Stir the mixture with your hands until completely covered. Cut a 2-foot piece of twine, fold it in half and knot the ends together. Mold a 3-inch ball of fruit/nut mixture over the knotted end. Repeat until all the mixture is used. Freeze until hardened then hang from a tree branch. Store the rest in a plastic storage bag in the freezer.

Baked Goods

Breads, Pasta, Cookies & Cakes

Buggie Bread Bake

1 c. flour
1 c. yellow corn meal
¾ tsp. salt
4 tsp. baking powder

¼ c. vegetable oil
1 c. milk
2 eggs with shells
½ c. Bag O' Bugs

Mix all dry ingredients. Stir in milk, eggs, and oil. Pour into a greased 9"x13" baking dish and bake at 350° for 20-25 minutes or until the toothpick comes out clean. Cool on a wire rack and cut into one-inch cubes, serve and store the remainder in a plastic bag.

Raisin-Nut Bread for Birds

Bluebirds, mockingbirds, robins, and thrushes, jays and woodpeckers.

2 c. whole-wheat flour
3 tsp. baking powder
1 ½ c. raisins
1 c. chopped nuts, any kind

1 c. milk
¼ c. vegetable oil
1 egg with shells

Stir together flour and baking powder. Add raisins and nuts. Mix milk, oil and eggs to combine. Pour into dry ingredients, and stir with fork until moist. Crush eggshells into small pieces and add to mixture. Pour into a greased bread pan; bake at 400° for 20 min. To serve, crumble small portions onto a table feeder.

75

Stuffing FOR the Birds

Bluebirds, chickadees, jays, mockingbirds,
nuthatches, titmice, woodpeckers and wrens.

½ loaf whole wheat bread (preferably organic)   ½ lb. hamburger, raw or cooked
½ c. cooking oil   ½ c. hulled sunflower seeds
½ c. raisins

Tear bread into small pieces. Combine all ingredients and mix. Serve in tray feeder.

Peanut Butter Pasta

8 oz. pasta or leftover pasta   ½ c. chopped peanuts
½ c. natural peanut butter   ½ c. raisins
¼ c. cooking oil

Cook pasta according to directions or use leftover pasta. Thoroughly mix peanut butter and oil, then toss with cooked pasta. Add chopped peanuts and raisins and mix well. Serve on a table feeder.

Leftover Pasta Quick Treat

pasta, cooked leftovers   cooking oil
1 can mixed fruit

Drain canned fruit. In a large bowl, mix any kind of leftover pasta with mixed fruit. Drizzle enough cooking oil to coat well. With a hand chopper or food processor, chop the pasta and fruit into small pieces and serve on a table feeder.

76

Pasta Pie for the Birds

Crows, jays, robins, starlings

8 oz uncooked spaghetti

¼ c. cooking oil

3 eggs with sells

½ c. shredded cheese

Cook spaghetti according to package directions, or use leftover cooked pasta. In a large bowl, combine cooked pasta with remaining ingredients. Crush egg sells into small pieces and add to mixture. Put into a greased, 8" x 8" baking dish and bake at 350° for 10 minutes. Slice into squares and serve on a low feeder or directly on the ground.

Note: you could add ¼ lb. hamburger to add a little more sustenance.

Blueberry Oat Bread

Bluebirds, catbirds, jays, mockingbirds, robins, thrushes and wrens.

1 ¼ c. boiling water

¾ c. oatmeal

1 c. blueberries, fresh or thawed

¼ molasses

3 tbs. cooking oil

1 pkg. dry active yeast

¼ c. warm water

4 c. whole wheat flour

Combine first five ingredients. Set aside and let cool. Sprinkle yeast into warm water in a large bowl, and stir until dissolved. Stir oatmeal mixture into yeast. Stir in 2 cups flour. Add remaining flour and knead with a mixer or by hand. Cover and put in a warm place to rise for 30 minutes. Beat dough down, and then spread into a greased loaf pan. Brush oil over the top, cover and let rise again, until about 1 inch from the top of the pan. Bake at 425° for 45 minutes. Cool on a wire rack. To serve, tear into small pieces to serve in an open tray feeder.

Orange Bread

Bluebirds, mockingbirds, robins, wrens and orioles, jays

2 ¼ c. whole wheat flour

½ c. sugar

2 tsp. baking powder

¼ c. melted butter

1 large orange

2 eggs, with shells

1 c. orange juice

Wash the orange well in mild soapy water and rinse. Zest 2 tbs. of the rind. Peel the orange and dice the pulp into small pieces. Stir together flour, sugar, and baking powder. In another bowl, whisk eggs with orange juice and add melted butter, fruit and orange zest, and stir well. Crush eggshells into small pieces and add to egg mixture. Add fruit and flour mixture to egg mixture then mix well until moist. Pour into greased 9"x5"x3" loaf pan, and bake at 350° for about 55 minutes. Cool on a wire rack, then slice off a piece and crumble onto a table feeder.

Birdie Goes Bananas Bread

Treat for chickadees, robins, jays,
mockingbirds, thrushes and wrens, woodpeckers

2 ½ c. whole wheat flour

3 tsp. baking powder

¾ c. brown sugar

¼ c. butter

2 eggs, with shell

6 ripe, mashed bananas

¼ c. milk

1 c. chopped nuts.

Combine flour and baking powder. In another bowl, beat together sugar, butter and egg. Crush eggshells into small pieces and add to bowl, mix in bananas and milk. Add flour mixture and stir until smooth. Stir in nuts. Pour into a greased 9"x5"x3" loaf pan, and bake at 350° for 65 minutes. Cool on a wire rack. Break into small pieces and serve daily portions on a table feeder. Store the remainder in a plastic storage bag in the refrigerator.

Note: If you leave out the eggshells, you *and* the birds can share this treat!

PB&J for the Birds

Bluebirds, chickadees, jays, mockingbirds, orioles, robins,
woodpeckers and wrens.

2 slices whole wheat bread   *jelly, fruit or berry*
Natural, chunky peanut butter   *½ c. wild birdseed mix*

Pour birdseed onto a plate. Spread a thick coating of peanut butter onto one
slice of bread then gently press peanut butter side down into the birdseed.
Cover the second slice of bread with grape jelly. Press slices together to make a
sandwich. Slice into 1 in. cubes. Serve on a feeder tray.

Bagels for the Birds

2 - 4 bagels, day old   *¼ c. raisins*
½ c. rendered suet or lard   *1 c. wild birdseed mix*
½ c. natural, crunchy peanut butter   *twine*

Mix suet or lard with peanut butter and spread over both sides of bagel. Chop
raisins into small pieces and put in a large plastic bag. Add the birdseed and toss
together. Put the bagel in the bag and shake well to coat. Cut a piece of twine
about 2 feet long and tie a loop through the hole in the bagel to hang outside.

Graham Cracker Treat

1 package of graham crackers   *½ c. millet*
½ c. natural peanut butter   *½ c. peanuts*
½ c. rendered suet   *½ c. safflower or sunflower seeds*

Combine all in a food processor, then process to a crumbly consistency. Chill
then serve on a table feeder. Store the rest in a marked plastic bag in the freezer.

Cornie Corn Crumble

2 c. yellow cornmeal
2 c. whole wheat flour
1 c. dried milk
4 tsp. baking powder
4 eggs including shells

1 c. cooked white rice
1 c. cracked corn
1 c. hulled millet
4 c. warm water
2 c. frozen corn (thawed)

Mix all dry ingredients together. Add wet ingredients. Grease a 9"x13" pan and bake at 425° for 25 minutes. Cool completely on a wire rack then crumble into medium size pieces. Serve on a table feeder or hang in a mesh bag. Store the remainder in a marked plastic bag in the refrigerator.

Seven-Grain Bird Bread

2 8 ½ oz. boxes Jiffy corn muffin mix
2 c. seven-grain cereal, uncooked

4 eggs with shells
1 c. natural peanut butter

Mix ingredients in a large bowl, adding enough water to make a cake-like batter. Pour into a greased 9"x13" baking dish. Bake at 350° for 30-35 minutes. Cool and then crumble onto a table feeder.

High Protein Bread

1 c. cornmeal
1 c. whole-wheat flour
4 tsp baking powder
½ c. peanut butter
¼ c. vegetable oil

2 eggs with shells
1 can high protein dog food
1 c. chopped nuts
1 c. milk
1 c. black-oil sunflower seeds

Mix all dry ingredients in large bowl and add milk, oil, eggs, dog food, peanut butter and nuts. Pour into a greased 9"x13" baking dish. Bake at 425° for 20-25 minutes. Cool and then crumble onto a table feeder or on the ground.

Sunny Blueberry Muffins

¼ c. hulled millet
1 c. milk
2 c. whole wheat flour
½ c. sugar
3 tsp. baking powder

½ tsp. salt
1 egg, lightly beaten
3 tbs. butter, melted
1 c. blueberries
1 c. hulled sunflower seeds

Grease muffin tins. Soak the millet in the milk for 10 minutes. Combine dry ingredients and sunflower seeds. Add egg and melted butter to the millet mixture. Stir in blueberries carefully. Combine with dry ingredients and mix well. Pour into muffing tins and bake at 400° for 25 minutes. Cool on a wire rack and crumble onto a table feeder.

Pancakes for the Birds

Blackbirds, bluebirds, dove, grackles, jays, mockingbirds, robins, starlings

1c. raisins   ¾ c. wild birdseed
Pancake mix to make 10-12 pancakes.

Prepare pancakes according to directions, adding strawberries and wild birdseed. Break up the pancakes or set out whole on a table feeder.

Seedy Corn Bread

2 c. yellow cornmeal
2 c. whole-wheat flour
1 c. dried milk
4 tsp. baking powder

4 eggs including shells
2 c. wild birdseed
1 c. uncooked oatmeal
4 c. warm water

Mix all dry ingredients together. Add wet ingredients and mix well. Pour into a greased 9"x13" pan and bake at 425° for 25 minutes. Cool completely on a wire rack then crumble pieces. Serve on a table feeder or hang in a mesh bag. Store the remained in a marked plastic bag in the refrigerator.

Fruit Bread

2 packages of yeast (2 tbs)
¼ c. warm water
¾ c. fruit juice
1 can mixed fruit

½ c. water
2 tbs. butter
7 c. of flour
½ c. raisins

Dissolve yeast in ¼c. warm water. Let yeast mixture sit while combining other ingredients, except flour. Stir yeast into juice mixture. Add flour, mixing first by spoon, then by hand. Turn out on floured surface and let rest about 10 min. Knead about 8 min., until surface is smooth and elastic. Divide into loaves and place in greased bread pans. Let rise until doubled in bulk. Bake at 425° for 25 to 30 minutes. Cool and serve in torn prices.

Red Berry Oat Cake

1 ¼ c. whole wheat flour
1 c. uncooked oatmeal
1 c. cornmeal
½ c. rendered suet or lard
1 egg

1 c. raspberries, strawberries
½ c. chopped nuts
1 c. milk
½ c. sugar

Stir together flour and cornmeal. Beat together suet and sugar; add egg and milk then beat well. Add dry ingredients to beaten mixture, beating until well combined. Crush eggshells into small pieces and add. Stir in oats, berries, nuts and eggshells. Pour into a greased and cake pan. Bake at 350° for about 1 hour. Let cool and break into chunks. Serve on table feeder or hang in a mesh bag.

Oatmeal Cookies for the Birds

1 c. whole-wheat flour
1 tsp baking powder
½ c. sugar
½ c. rendered suet, lard or butter

2 eggs, including shells
2 tbs. milk
1 c. rolled oats
1 ½ c. wild birdseed

Stir together flour and baking powder. Beat together suet and sugar; add eggs, milk and beat well. Add dry ingredients to beaten mixture, beating until well combined. Crush eggshells into small pieces. Stir in oats, ¾-cup birdseed, and egg shells. Form into 1-inch balls and roll into remaining birdseed. Place on an cookie sheet. Bake at 375° for 10 to 12 minutes.

Raisin Oak Seed Cake

½ c. whole wheat bread crumbs
½ c. rolled oats, uncooked
½ c. whole milk
1 egg (include shell)

2 tbs. molasses
½ c. raisins
1 tbs. cooking oil
½ c. wild bird seed

Mix all Ingredients together and blend well. Pour mixture into a greased pie pan and bake at 350° for 30 minutes or until mixture is golden brown. Cool on a wire rack and then crumble pie onto a tray feeder.

Berry Betty

1 c. sugar
½ c. strawberries
½ c. raspberries
½ c. shortening
½ c. water

2 c. whole wheat flour
1 tsp. baking soda
½ tsp. baking powder
½ c. chopped nuts

Mix flour, baking powder, soda and nutmeats. Set aside. Boil sugar, berries, shortening and water for 5 minutes. Add liquid to dry ingredients. Pour onto a greased 8"x8" pan. Bake at 350° for 20-25 minutes. Cool in a wire rack then cut into pieces and serve on feeder tray or ground feeder.

Raspberry Muffins

1 c. cornmeal
¾ c. raspberries
1 c. whole-wheat flour
½ c. rendered suet or bacon drippings

1 c. whole- wheat breadcrumbs
¼ tsp. sand
1 tsp. baking soda
1 c. water

Combine cornmeal, flour, breadcrumbs and soda in a medium bowl. Add raspberries and sand. Melt suet in the microwave. Pour in melted suet and water. Mix well and then spoon into muffin tins. Bake at 350° for 15 minutes. Serve on table feeder or hang in a mesh bag.

Nutty Oak Seed Cake

½ c. whole wheat bread crumbs
½ c. rolled oats, uncooked
½ c. whole milk
½ c. chopped nuts

2 tbs. molasses
1 egg (include shell)
1 tbs. cooking oil
½ c. wild bird seed

Mix all Ingredients together and blend well. Pour mixture into a greased pie pan and bake at 350° for 30 minutes or until mixture is golden brown. Crumble pie and place in feeder.

Apple Nut Muffins

1 ½ c. whole wheat flour
½ c. corn meal
½ c. millet
3 tsp baking powder
1 ½ c. thawed apple juice concentrate

2 eggs , with shells
½ c. dried apples, chopped
½ c. chopped pine nuts
½ c. dry milk
1 tbs. cooking oil

Stir together flour, cornmeal, millet and baking powder. Mix together eggs and oil, dry milk and apple juice concentrate. Add dry ingredients to egg mixture, beating until well combined. Crush eggshells into small pieces and chop dried apples into small pieces. Stir in dried apples, nuts and eggshells. Spoon batter into muffin cups. Bake at 350° for 15-20 minutes. Serve on table feeder or place in a mesh bag and hang.

Decorative Bird Feed

Pinecone Feeder Treat

2 c. rendered suet
2 c. natural, chunky peanut butter
½ c whole-wheat breadcrumbs
½ c. hulled sunflower seeds
½ c. whole-wheat flour
½ c. unsalted nuts
several large pinecones

½ c. quick oats
¼ c. millet
¼ c. raisins
¼ c. dried apples, chopped small
½ c. wild birdseed
½ c. sugar

Melt suet in a saucepan over low heat. Add peanut butter, stirring until melted and well blended. Mix the rest of the ingredients together in a large bowl. Allow the suet-peanut butter blend to cool until slightly thickened, and then stir it into the mixture in the bowl. Press the mixture between the "petals" of the pinecones. Wrap a thin wire or tie some twine around the end of the pinecone. Place in the refrigerator until firm. Hang from a feeder pole or the branches of trees.

Corn Cob Bunches

Take a several fresh ears of corn that are still in the husk. Peel the husks back and remove the silk. Bunch several of these together and tie the husks together just above the corncob. Hang on feeder pole or in a tree or use as a decoration on your home.

Hanging Log Feeder

½ c. rendered suet

½ c. natural peanut butter

1 c. wild bird seed

½ c. raisins

Use a 1' x 3" diameter log or piece of untreated wood. Drill several 1" holes in it. Screw an "eye" into the top to hang with a piece of twine. Melt suet and peanut butter in a pan. Let cool slightly then add birdseed and raisins, then mix well. Push the soft suet in the holes and hang on a feeder pole or from a tree branch. The log can be reused again and again by simply adding more suet mixture.

Hanging String Sweets & Treats

popped popcorn

peanuts

pecan halves

walnut halves

dried plums

dried dates

cotton string

fresh cranberries

raisins

dried apple slices

orange slices

dried apricots

Choose from the list of ingredients above or use them all to make a pretty and edible decorations to hang from the trees. Cut cotton string into 2-foot lengths and tie a small twig to the end to prevent fruit and nuts from sliding off. Use a large needle to string pieces of dried fruit, nuts and popcorn in a decorative pattern onto the cotton string. During the holidays, add some colorful ribbons to the ends to make them extra special.

Orange Suet Cups

2 c. rendered suet

2 c. natural, chunky peanut butter

½ c whole-wheat breadcrumbs

½ c. hulled sunflower seeds

½ c. whole-wheat flour

½ c. unsalted nuts

several oranges

½ c. quick oats

¼ c. millet

¼ c. raisins

½ c. cornmeal

½ c. wild birdseed

½ c. sugar

pipe cleaners

Melt suet in a saucepan over low heat. Add peanut butter, stirring until melted and well blended. Cut oranges in half and hollow out orange halves. Put the pulp into a large bowl and add the rest of the ingredients; mix well. Allow the suet-peanut butter blend to cool until slightly thickened, and then stir it into the mixture in the bowl. Poke a hole on each side of the orange half new the top. Work one end of the pipe cleaner through each hole, bending the ends to make handles with which to hang the cup. Fill the empty haves with suet mixture and hang outside.

Pretty Popcorn Birdie Garland

popped popcorn

peanuts

pecan halves

walnut halves

dried plums

dried dates

cotton string

fresh cranberries

raisins

dried apple slices

orange slices

dried apricots

Choose from the list of ingredients above or use them all to make a pretty and edible garland for the birds. Use a large needle to string pieces of dried fruit, nuts and popcorn in a decorative pattern onto the cotton string. Drape them in trees or on fences; wherever you please outside.

I ♥ Birds!

1 c. natural peanut butter
flat wooden heart (or any wooden shape)
4 feet of ¼-inch wide ribbon

2 c. wild birdseed
drill

Drill one small hole in the center of each side of the top of the heart. Cut two lengths of ribbon, each 2-foot long and run a piece of ribbon through each hole and knot the ends. Cover the wooden heart completely with a thick layer of peanut butter. Pour the birdseed onto a plate and then place the heart in the birdseed and completely cover both sides of the heart with the birdseed. Tie the ends of ribbon together in a bow over a tree branch to hang.

A Berry Seedy Wreath

1-foot square of rabbit wire.
1 pkt. clear gelatin
¼ c. whole-wheat flour
2-foot length of ribbon

2-foot length of wire
4 c. wild birdseed
several sprigs of berries

Use wire cutters to cut a wreath shape, 10-inches in diameter from rabbit wire. Mix gelatin, according to directions. Pour seeds & nuts into gelatin and mix well. Add more seeds if mixture does not hold together. Mold onto the wire frame. Attach sprigs of berries with wire and hang with a festive ribbon.

Sunny Bunches for the Birds

Trim several sunflowers 1½-foot from the head and secure in a bunch with wire. Hang from the branches of tress, put in window boxes or use to decorate the outside of your home.

Fruit & Nut Tree for the Birds

6" foam ball	dried wheat grass
A 6-9" terracotta pot	dried apricots
Glue gun	dried figs
Rocks	2 c. wild birdseed
Wire	4 apples
1 c. peanuts in the shell	2 oranges

Slice apples and oranges into ¼-inch slices. Wire fruit together by piercing several slices with a wire and twisting it securely, leaving a 3-inch wire stem. Do the same with the rest of the fruit, peanuts and dried wheat grass. Cut a section of branch or strong vine to form the trunk and hot glue to the bottom of the terracotta pot. Secure in place with several small rocks, filling to within an inch from the top of the pot. Cut a paper plate to the same diameter as the pot and then cut a hole in the center. Slide the paper plate over the branch and press down until it rests on top of the rocks. Cut a hole in the foam ball and hot glue the ball onto the top of the branch. Insert wired branches of wheat heads into the foam ball, evenly spacing them as you work around the entire ball. Add the wired bunches of fruit and peanuts to fill the entire ball. Pour the wild birdseed onto the paper plate and fill to the rim of the terracotta pot. Place out on your deck for you and the birds to enjoy.

Wheat or Oat Grass Wreaths

Gather several bundles of wheat or oat grass. Use a small gauge wire to secure several small (about a handful) clusters together and hang them upside down to dry out (for a day or two). Trim the ends of each cluster to about 3-inches below the wire and secure one cluster to the wreath frame. Fasten another cluster on the frame so that the grassy tops cover the wire securing the first bunch. Continue adding clusters in this manner until the wreath is complete. Fasten a piece of wire on the back of the wreath to hang. Put outside in an area where the birds can easily get to it.

Notes

Notes

Notes

Notes

Notes